Chords Made Easy →

WRITTEN BY TOM FLEMING

Amsco Publications
A Part of The **Music Sales Group**
New York/London/Paris/Sydney/Copenhagen/Berlin/Tokyo/Madrid

Cover photography by Peter Svarzbein, assisted by Greg Wilson
Models: Ethan Campbell, Canyon, Sonia De Los Santos,
Megan Leach, and Akil (Myself) Omari
Cover design by Josh Labouve

CD credits:
All guitars: Tom Fleming
Bass: Neil Williams
Drums: Brett Morgan
Recorded & mixed by Jonas Persson and John Rose

Project editor: David Bradley
Interior design and layout by Len Vogler

*Thanks to Heather Ramage for her understanding and patience,
and to Rick Cardinali for all the tea and cakes.*

Order No. AM 982355
International Standard Book Number: 0.8256.3455.5

Exclusive Distributors:
Music Sales Corporation
257 Park Avenue South, New York, NY 10010 USA
Music Sales Limited
8/9 Frith Street, London W1D 3JB England
Music Sales Pty. Limited
120 Rothschild Street, Rosebery, Sydney, NSW 2018, Australia

Printed in the United States of America by
Vicks Lithograph and Printing Corporation

Table of Contents

CD track listing 4

Introduction 5

A word about tuning. 6

Basic chord construction and terms. 7

What Is a Chord?. 7

Thirds. 7

Fifths. 8

Sevenths. 8

Steps of the Scale and Roman Numerals. 9

Basic Chords 9

Let's begin at the beginning. 11

Bobbing 11

Old Faithful 11

III's a Crowd 12

Living for Today 12

Show You Something 13

C Change 13

Cycling 14

The cycle of fifths. 15

The II–V–I progression 16

Semi-Jazz-Tastic 16

Chord construction 17

But I don't want to play jazz. 18

A Note on Technique 19

All about the blues 20

Beginner's Blues No. 1 20

Beginner's Blues No. 2 20

Beginner's Blues No. 3 21

Advanced Beginner's Blues 22

Fruit Smoothie 22

All Is Well 23

Adding flavor 24

Big Bossa Man 25

Let's Swing Again 25

Dirty Dozen 26

Stop Bossing 26

It's not natural. 28

The art of tension management. 29

Basic Bossa 29

Natural Bossa 30

Unnatural Bossa 30

Cookin' Bossa 31

Bar chords: the inevitable chapter. 32

Bar chords in action 34

Slippery Punk. 34

Coalface Piano Disaster 34

Sweet 'n' High 35

Behind Bars 35

When Gary Met Larry. 36

Mooning. 36

More fancy jazz. 37

Natural-Tension Blues 38

Altered-Tension Blues 38

Minor Quibble. 39

Latin Homework 40

Inversions 41

All Joined Up 41

Forward Slash 42

Suspensions 43

Hangin' On 43

Signing Off. 44

The harmonized major scale 45

Jazz Voicings (root–7th–3rd–5th) 45

Jazz Voicings (root–3rd–7th–9th) 45

Semi-Jazz Voicings (root–5th–7th–3rd) 46

Transposition chart 47

Suggested reading. 48

Track

1. Tuning Track — page 6
2. Bobbing (demo) — page 11
3. Bobbing (backing) — page 11
4. Old Faithful (demo) — page 11
5. Old Faithful (backing) — page 11
6. III's a Crowd (demo) — page 12
7. III's a Crowd (backing) — page 12
8. Living for Today (demo) — page 12
9. Living for Today (backing) — page 12
10. Show You Something (demo) — page 13
11. Show You Something (backing) — page 13
12. C Change (demo) — page 13
13. C Change (backing) — page 13
14. Cycling (demo) — page 14
15. Cycling (backing) — page 14
16. Semi-Jazz-Tastic (demo) — page 16
17. Semi-Jazz-Tastic (backing) — page 16
18. Beginner's Blues No. 1 (demo) — page 20
19. Beginner's Blues No. 1 (backing) — page 20
20. Beginner's Blues No. 2 (demo) — page 20
21. Beginner's Blues No. 2 (backing) — page 20
22. Beginner's Blues No. 3 (demo) — page 21
23. Beginner's Blues No. 3 (backing) — page 21
24. Advanced Beginner's Blues (demo) — page 22
25. Advanced Beginner's Blues (backing) — page 22
26. Fruit Smoothie (demo) — page 22
27. Fruit Smoothie (backing) — page 22
28. All Is Well (demo) — page 23
29. All Is Well (backing) — page 23
30. Big Bossa Man (demo) — page 25
31. Big Bossa Man (backing) — page 25
32. Let's Swing Again (demo) — page 25
33. Let's Swing Again (backing) — page 25
34. Dirty Dozen (demo) — page 26
35. Dirty Dozen (backing) — page 26
36. Stop Bossing (demo) — page 26
37. Stop Bossing (backing) — page 26
38. Basic Bossa (demo) — page 29

Track

39. Basic Bossa (backing) — page 29
40. Natural Bossa (demo) — page 30
41. Natural Bossa (backing) — page 30
42. Unnatural Bossa (demo) — page 30
43. Unnatural Bossa (backing) — page 30
44. Cookin' Bossa (demo) — page 31
45. Cookin' Bossa (backing) — page 31
46. Slippery Punk (demo) — page 34
47. Slippery Punk (backing) — page 34
48. Coalface Piano Disaster (demo) — page 34
49. Coalface Piano Disaster (backing) — page 34
50. Sweet 'n' High (demo) — page 35
51. Sweet 'n' High (backing) — page 35
52. Behind Bars (demo) — page 35
53. Behind Bars (backing) — page 35
54. When Gary Met Larry (demo) — page 36
55. When Gary Met Larry (backing) — page 36
56. Mooning (demo) — page 36
57. Mooning (backing) — page 36
58. Natural-Tension Blues (demo) — page 38
59. Natural-Tension Blues (backing) — page 38
60. Altered-Tension Blues (demo) — page 38
61. Altered-Tension Blues (backing) — page 38
62. Minor Quibble (demo) — page 39
63. Minor Quibble (backing) — page 39
64. Latin Homework (demo—slow) — page 40
65. Latin Homework (backing—slow) — page 40
66. Latin Homework (demo—fast) — page 40
67. Latin Homework (backing—fast) — page 40
68. All Joined Up (demo) — page 41
69. All Joined Up (backing) — page 41
70. Forward Slash (demo) — page 42
71. Forward Slash (backing) — page 42
72. Hangin' On (demo) — page 43
73. Hangin' On (backing) — page 43
74. Signing Off (demo) — page 44
75. Signing Off (backing) — page 44

This book is intended as a brief exploration of the world of guitar chords and all sorts of ways in which they can be strung together. I've assumed that you can find your way around the instrument and understand chord boxes. This book is not heavy on theory. If you find some of the terms puzzling, there are plenty of excellent books available on general music theory. My aim is to help you open up your ears to some new possibilities—where you go from there is up to you.

Each chord sequence is presented as two tracks on the CD: first, as a demonstration track (with guitar), and second, as a backing track (without guitar) for you to practice with. You can, of course, use the backing tracks for any purpose; most of them use bass and drums only, so you can try varying the chords. The key thing here, as ever, is to *listen to what you are playing*. If it sounds good, it is good. Simple!

The chord boxes in this book do not dictate which fingers to use, however, the accompanying photos show the most common fingerings. Some chords can be played in a number of different ways; for others, there is really only one sensible fingering.

We'll start with some really simple sequences. Feel free to skip ahead if you think you've covered this ground before.

A word about tuning

"What's with this guy? I know how to tune a guitar. Give me a break!"

OK, maybe you do. But, to my ears at least, a lot of players sound *very nearly but not quite* in tune. The difference may be tiny, but it does make a big difference.

Of course, occasionally there just isn't time. If you're playing a one-hour party set with little or no break between songs, you just have to "wing it." In this situation it helps to have a guitar that holds its tuning, and a good stage tuner.

If you're tuning by ear (and I often find that electronic tuners don't *quite* get there), there are several methods to choose from but, oddly enough, the one we all learn first is actually the best:

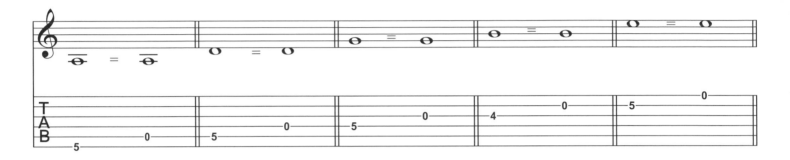

After this basic tuning, check the following octaves:

- high E string, 7th fret against open B string—adjust B string
- high E string, 3rd fret against open G string—adjust G string
- B string, 3rd fret against open D string—adjust D string
- G string, 2nd fret against open A string—adjust A string
- D string, 2nd fret against open E string—adjust E string

Finally, check the top and bottom E strings. If they don't sound perfectly in tune, go back to the top of this procedure until you find the error.

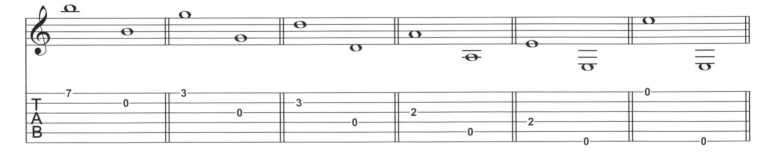

Don't be tempted to use harmonics. The modern guitar has to be tuned to *equal temperament*. Harmonics produce mathematically *pure* intervals, which actually sound better in their own right, but are unfortunately incompatible with the guitar's fret spacing.

For now, tune your guitar (from low to high) to **Track 1** on the accompanying CD.

What Is a Chord?

A *chord* is the sound made when two or more notes are sounded together. They don't even have to be played on the same instrument—merely at the same time. When you play two or more notes together on the guitar, or two or more people play or sing different notes, you hear a chord.

Even though two-note chords can be useful and effective, Western harmony in general is founded on three-note chords. Until the nineteenth century, four-note chords were only used in specific circumstances governed by strict rules. Today, chords of four notes or more are found in almost all styles of music, including blues, jazz, rock, pop, and contemporary classical music.

Although there are only a few types of three-note chords, the possibilities multiply rapidly as we add notes. The resulting complexity can be bewildering at times, but the reward is in the almost limitless palette of sounds at our disposal once we string these chords together into progressions. How? You may love the sound of a 9♯11 chord, but what should come afterwards? This book explores some of these questions, but without blinding you with science. The emphasis here is on listening and learning by example.

Before we get into the main business of the book, let's look at a few basic concepts that you'll need to know about to make the most of it. I'm assuming that you're familiar with the basic nuts and bolts of music theory, such as note names, tones and semitones, the major scale, and the treble clef. It's worth spending some time looking at a few of these theoretical building blocks first. Then we can get stuck into chords and chord sequences without constant explanation.

Thirds

Chords are generally, but not always, constructed using intervals known as *thirds*. Even chords that look as though they contain many different complex intervals can usually be analyzed in terms of thirds.

A *third* is the interval between two notes which are three note names apart, including the notes themselves. So C–E (C–D–E), D–F (D–E–F), and G–B♭ (G–A–B♭) are all thirds.

You need to know about two different types of thirds: *major* and *minor*. The easiest way to remember these is that the *major third,* as its name suggests, is a *bigger* interval than the minor third. In fact, the major third is an interval of four semitones, or two whole tones, whereas the *minor third* is a tone and a half, or three semitones.

Most chords can be thought of as being constructed by adding thirds together. For example, if we take the notes C and E (a major third, as we have seen) and the next third (G), we get a major chord or *triad*. Adding the next third (B) gives us a four-note chord (C major 7).

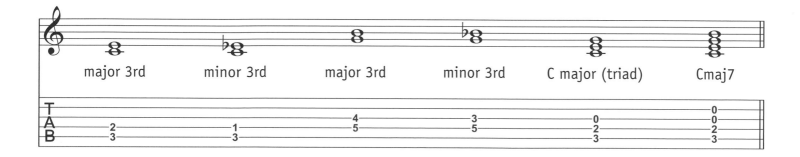

major 3rd   minor 3rd   major 3rd   minor 3rd   C major (triad)   Cmaj7

Fifths

We also need to consider these new notes in relation to the root of the chord. The interval here between C and G is known as a *fifth* because it spans five note names: C–D–E–F–G. There are three types of fifths which you need to know about: *perfect, diminished,* and *augmented.* A perfect fifth is the interval between the first and fifth steps of the major scale, or three tones and a semitone (or seven semitones). Diminished and augmented fifths contain one less and one more semitone, respectively:

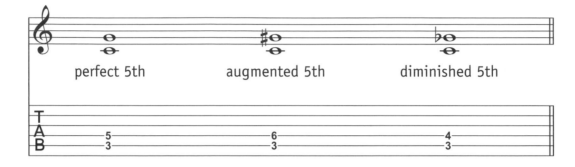

Sevenths

The fourth note of the Cmaj7 chord above is a *seventh* from the root. There are two types of sevenths that you need to know about. The *major seventh* is the interval between the first and seventh notes of the major scale. (It's easier to think of it as one semitone less than an octave.) If we shrink this by another semitone we get a *minor seventh,* often known as a *flat seventh:*

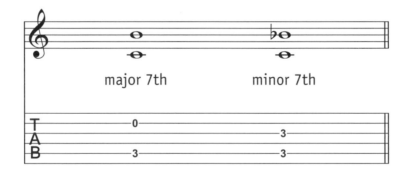

In this book, we will often look at exactly how a chord is constructed in terms of these intervals from the root. The major scale is taken as the norm, so "1–3–5–7" refers to the root, third, fifth, and seventh of the major scale (root, major third, perfect fifth, and major seventh). "1–♭3–5–♭7" departs from this by lowering (*flatting*) both the third and seventh, giving us the root, minor third, perfect fifth, and minor seventh.

Steps of the Scale and Roman Numerals

We can use either theoretical terms or roman numerals to refer to the steps of the scale (scale degrees) and the chords built upon them.

Later, we will use these terms and numerals to refer to chords such as "V7," meaning a 7th chord built on the fifth step of the scale, also known as the *dominant 7th*.

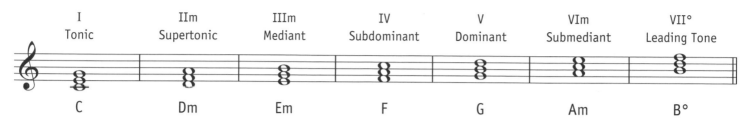

I	IIm	IIIm	IV	V	VIm	VII°
Tonic	Supertonic	Mediant	Subdominant	Dominant	Submediant	Leading Tone
C	Dm	Em	F	G	Am	B°

Basic Chords

For the first part of the book, before we get into anything tricky, I'm going to assume that you know the following easy chords. If not, now's the time to brush up!

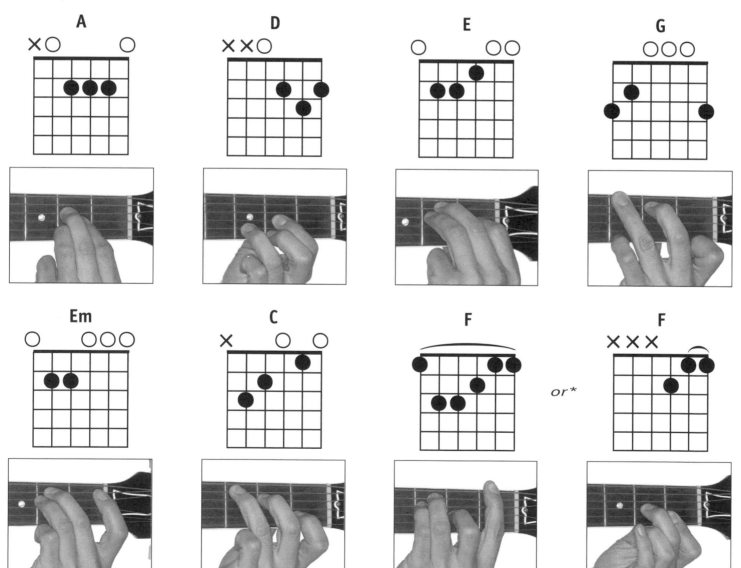

*The first version of the F chord is a *bar chord* (see page 32). If you find this difficult, you can use the second version for now—just make sure you don't play the bottom strings!

E7

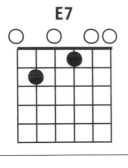

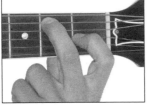

Am

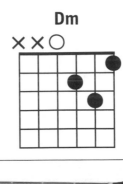

Dm

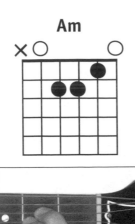

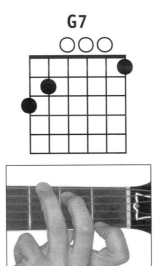

A7

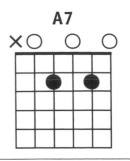

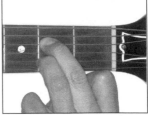

D7

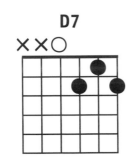

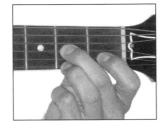

G7

It's a very good place to start. We're going to look at a few simple chord progressions that were probably among the first things you learned to play. You may not have looked too deeply at what was actually happening before, so we'll revisit these simple sequences before we take them further.

Bobbing CD tracks 2 & 3

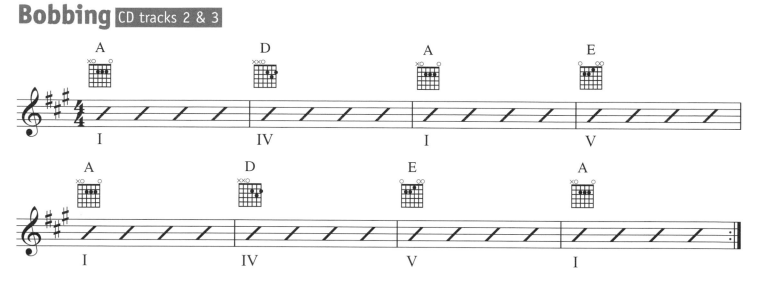

What's going on here then? This chord sequence is in the key of A (shown by the *key signature*), and the roman numerals I, IV, and V represent chords built on the tonic (A), subdominant (D), and dominant (E) scale degrees. These roman numerals are actually incredibly useful, as they give you an instant transposition method. You may have used a capo to transpose chord sequences without realizing that you can transpose a simple song into an easier key without knowing a lot of theory or hurting your fingers with impossible chord shapes. How? Simply refer to the **Transposition Chart** on page 47. This will instantly tell you that to play chords I, IV, and V you need C, F, and G (in C major) or D, G, and A (in D major), and so on. Could it be any easier?

Here's another simple sequence that's been used in hundreds of songs:

Old Faithful CD tracks 4 & 5

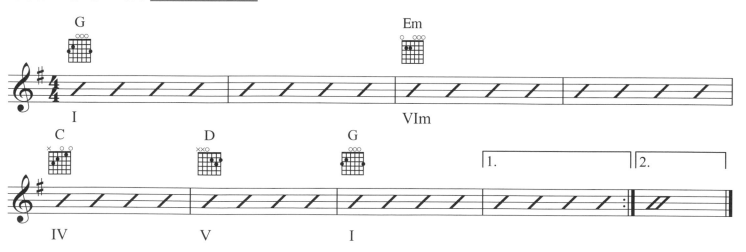

You'll notice chords I, IV, and V are still with us, this time in the key of G. The new chord adding interest in this sequence is the VIm chord. Try transposing this sequence into the keys of C, D, and A. On the guitar, this does more than merely change the key; each key sounds quite different because of the different open chords used. If you were writing a song using a simple sequence like this, you might play around with a few keys until you find one that suits the mood of the song, as well as your vocal range.

Let's add another chord to our vocabulary: IIIm. In the key of C, this is an E minor chord.

III's a Crowd CD tracks 6 & 7

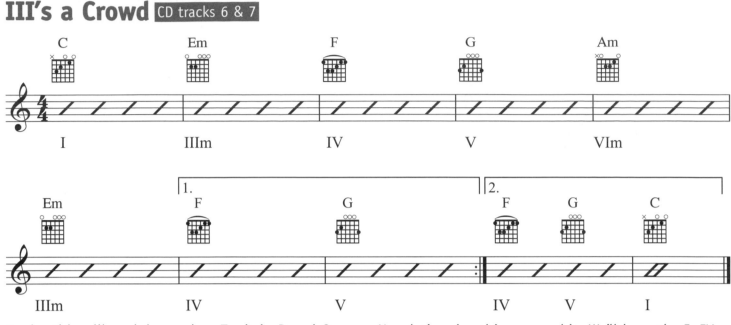

Again, this will work in any key. Try it in D and G using the transposition chart on page 47.

Now let's spice things up a bit. We'll keep the I, IV, V, and VIm chords the same but turn the IIIm chord into a dominant 7th chord. More about this below; let's hear it first:

Living for Today CD tracks 8 & 9

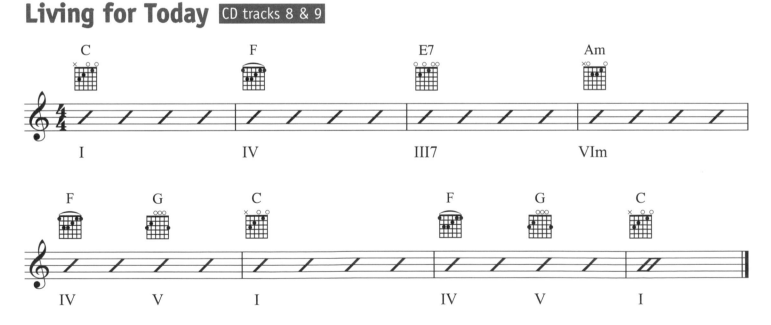

What's the difference between Em and E7? The most important difference is that the third is raised by a semitone. The E7 chord is basically a major chord with an added seventh. If you know a bit of theory, you may realize that it contains a note that does not belong to the key (G♯). This is called a *chromatic note* (from the Latin *chroma, meaning* "color"), and the chord is therefore a *chromatic chord*. It's

actually leading the ear away from C major toward the key of A minor, which is where the G♯ comes from. For now, just remember it as a useful color. You can still cheerfully use the transposition chart to play this sequence in other keys, as long as you remember to turn the IIIm chord into a dominant 7th chord.

Our look at the basic chords in the major key is nearly complete. To round it off, let's have a look at the IIm chord in action. We'll stay in C major, so we'll need a D minor chord.

Show You Something CD tracks 10 & 11

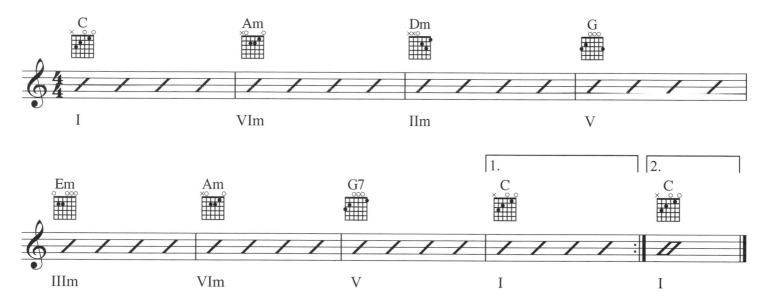

Now let's turn IIm and VIm and into dominant 7ths. And why not the V chord while we're at it? The chromatic note in chord VI7 is the C♯, which belongs to the key of D. I'll explain this in more detail shortly...

C Change CD tracks 12 & 13

The chromatic chord II7 (D7) is particularly effective if you've used some chromatic or unusual chords and want to lead the ear back to the dominant (V) and ultimately back to the tonic (I), as in the last two measures. It's called the *secondary dominant* because it is the V chord (dominant) of the V chord (dominant).

Cycling CD tracks 14 & 15

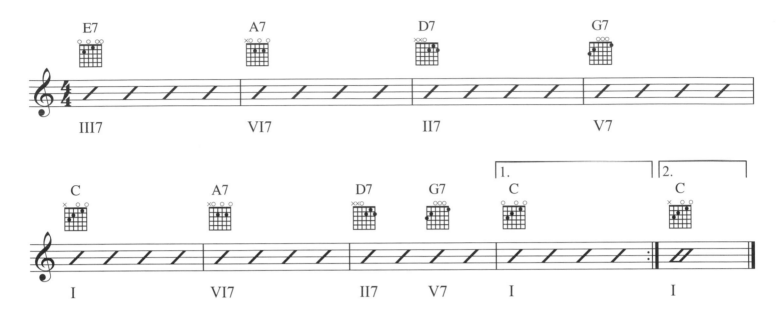

E7	A7	D7	G7
III7	VI7	II7	V7

C	A7	D7	G7	1. C	2. C
I	VI7	II7	V7	I	I

I'm sure you've spotted that we've turned our VIm chord (Am) into a dominant 7th as well. Where will all this end? Well, the type of chord progression we've established here is so strong that there's really no limit. You may suspect that as we move through chords III7–VI7–II7–V7, it sounds as though exactly the same thing is happening each time, and you'd be right. Just as chord II7 is called the secondary dominant, I suppose we could call VI7 the *tertiary dominant,* and so on (although no one ever does). This type of movement is called a *cycle of fifths* because the root of each chord is a fifth apart from the next. A cycle of fifths doesn't have to use dominant 7th chords, but they have a very strong sound and this sequence is common in jazz and pop music alike. Check out the middle section of Gershwin's "I Got Rhythm" for the perfect example.

In fact, movement in fifths is so strong and so common that you'll find it all throughout this book. Let's have a closer look at it now, so you'll know it when you see (or hear) it.

The sequence (if you can call two chords a sequence) of V to I is absolutely central to most Western music. In classical music it is called a *perfect cadence*. There are other types of cadences, but the perfect cadence is the most important, as the name suggests. It's the one you hear about sixteen times at the end of a Mozart symphony (or about fifty times at the end of a Beethoven symphony!), but the majority of pop and jazz tunes use it too. The effect is of resolution: the dominant chord (V), which may or may not contain a seventh, *wants* to resolve to the tonic (I).

This effect is so strong that a dominant 7th chord (a major chord with a lowered seventh) can be used effectively to bring about a change of key, whether temporarily or permanently. In classical terms, this is called a *modulation*. The cycle of fifths you've just heard is really a series of modulations, but each time we think we're going to arrive at a new key center, we're already on our way to yet another one—the ear expects a tonic chord but never gets one. Don't worry if you don't understand some of this yet. All will become clear as you progress through this book.

As so many chord sequences use repeated root movement in fifths (and they won't necessarily be chromatic chords as in the example above; the effect is still strong if all the chords belong to the same key), it's a good idea to be familiar with the whole cycle. Sometimes it is easier to think of a V–I progression as representing movement *up by a fourth* (rather than down by a fifth). It's fewer notes to count, for one thing.

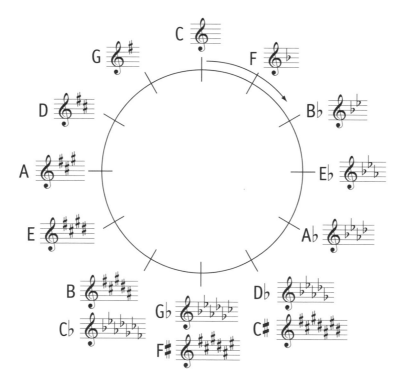

This useful diagram merely points out that C to F, for example, is a movement of a perfect fifth down or perfect fourth up and will therefore give you the root notes for a perfect cadence in that (the latter) key; likewise D to G, B♭ to E♭, F♯ to B, and so on.

This is an incredibly useful cycle to know, for all sorts of reasons. If you're familiar with the way key signatures work, for example, you will probably have seen it before, and it brings us conveniently to the next topic...

This is one of the most common chord progressions in jazz and pop music. We'll really get our teeth into it later in the book; for now let's have a quick look and move on.

Semi-Jazz-Tastic CD tracks 16 & 17

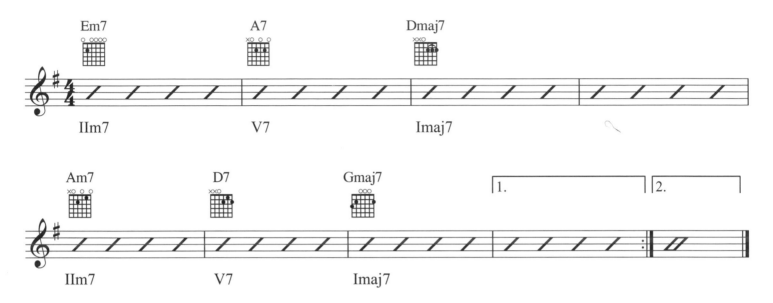

What's going on here then? Briefly, we've got a II–V–I in the key of D, followed by a II–V–I in the key of G. As we have seen, the perfect cadence (V–I) is an effective means of establishing a key center. If we prepare the ground with the II chord from the same key, the effect is even more pronounced. Each of these II–V–I progressions uses

diatonic chords only (*diatonic* being the opposite of chromatic, i.e., belonging to the key). As we have already seen, a diatonic II chord in the major key is *always* minor and the V chord is *always* major (with or without sevenths, as above), so the ear is left in no doubt of the key center we've reached—if only temporarily, which is often the case.

We've gotten this far using what you might call *open* chords—these are generally the first chords a guitarist learns, and will get you a long way in many styles of music. Many famous players never move beyond them (and who am I to lecture Bob Dylan on his choice of chords?), but as this book is about *understanding* chord progressions as well as playing them, let's dig a little deeper into building chords from scratch.

Open chords tend to use the first few frets of the guitar and a few open strings (obviously!). This makes them relatively easy to play and guarantees a good "ringy" sound once you've got the basic

technique. The drawbacks of these shapes are that they are not always *voiced* well (I'm referring to the way the notes are arranged inside the chord) and that they are not *moveable:* you can move the shape itself, but the open strings will stay at the same pitch, so the notes within the chord may clash. This can sound fantastic, of course, but we need to find ways of creating chords that are both well-voiced *and* moveable.

Let's have a look at some of these open chords before we move on to more advanced things. Here's an ordinary C major chord:

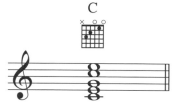

As we saw earlier, a C major triad contains three notes (C, E, and G), yet this C major shape contains five notes. This is because two of the notes of the triad are *doubled:* the root (C) and third (E) each occur twice, the fifth (G) only once.

Contrast this with the classic open shape for E major:

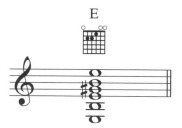

Here, the root (E) occurs three times, the fifth (B) twice and the third (G♯) only once. Is it any wonder that playing in different keys using these chord shapes results in such different sounds?

As you develop as a guitarist, you will probably always use these simple shapes to some degree.

They are easy to reach for, do the job simply, and give a good ringy sound, especially on an acoustic guitar. I'm not trying to give the cold shoulder to these shapes, but if you broaden your approach to include moveable chords, the world will be your harmonic oyster.

But I don't want to play jazz...

Many of the chords in this chapter may seem distinctly jazzy. As any guitar teacher will tell you, not everyone wants to play jazz, so why am I about to take you on a whirlwind tour of jazz harmony as applied to the guitar? First, you'd be surprised at the amount of jazz harmony that finds its way into contemporary pop, soul, R&B, and even house music; second, jazz is in many ways the most complex music around, and if I can equip you with the basic set of tools to deal with jazz, you'll breeze your way through most other chord progressions. Are you convinced? Of course, you may be really interested in jazz anyway, in which case you're already onboard.

Let's get away from the "kitchen sink" approach of open chords and consider the following question: In a complex musical language such as jazz (or any of the others listed above, stay with me...), which notes are essential to a chord and which notes can be left out?

The answer may surprise you. In a musical language consisting mainly of 7th chords of one kind or another, the essential notes are the third and seventh. The fifth is much less important, and although we'll generally be including the root for the moment, as soon as you get into a situation where there's a bass player, you can generally leave that out too. Don't worry about why for the moment...

Let's look at just three basic chord types: major 7th (maj7), dominant 7th (7), and minor 7th (m7). I'm going to show you two shapes for each of these, and with these six chord shapes you will be able to get through about three quarters of all the jazz standards ever written, not to mention all those other styles. The first three have the root on the sixth string, the second three on the fifth string.

Roots on the Sixth String

Roots on the Fifth String

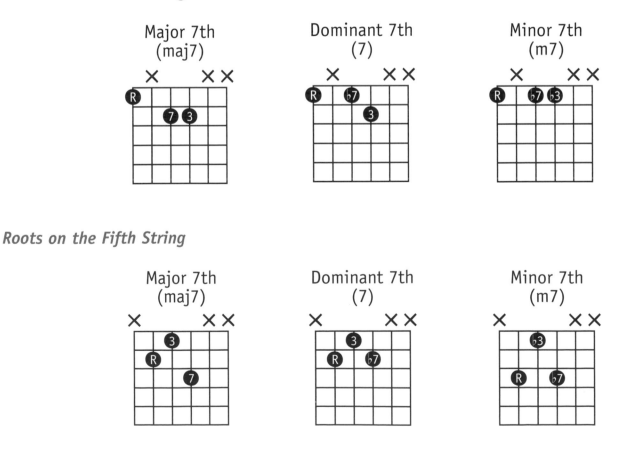

These shapes are moveable, so all you have to do to use them is find the root note on the appropriate string and play the desired shape with the root (R) occurring at that fret.

But how will I know where to find the root?

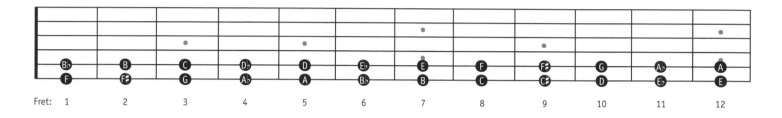

Fret: 1   2   3   4   5   6   7   8   9   10   11   12

As you can see, a C7 chord could have its root on the sixth string (eighth fret) or on the fifth string (third fret).

But how do I know which string to use for the root?

If you don't already know the notes at every fret of the instrument *(tsk, tsk)*, then use this handy root finder for the fifth and sixth strings:

Simple: for now, *always* use the minimum amount of hand movement. So, if you were playing a song using just Gm7 and C7, either of these two possibilities would work well:

But either of these would be inelegant, because of the larger movement involved:

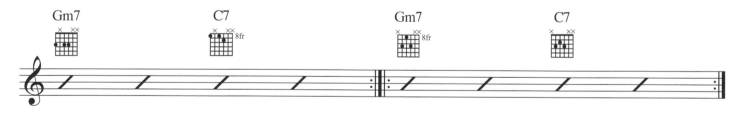

A Note on Technique

You may have noticed the number of muted strings in these shapes (marked **X**). It's easy to avoid these strings when playing fingerstyle, but most of the following sequences sound better strummed. How can you play nice big rhythmic strums without a lot of open strings ringing? The answer is just to let your fingers (and thumb) mute the strings you don't want to hear while allowing the strings you do want to hear ring out. In other words, the sort of "lazy" technique that you must avoid when playing open chords is exactly what you want here!

Now let's put these shapes into practice. The following progressions use these basic shapes all over the neck.

All about the blues

What better way to put these new shapes to use than with a simple 12-bar blues?

Beginner's Blues No. 1 CD tracks 18 & 19

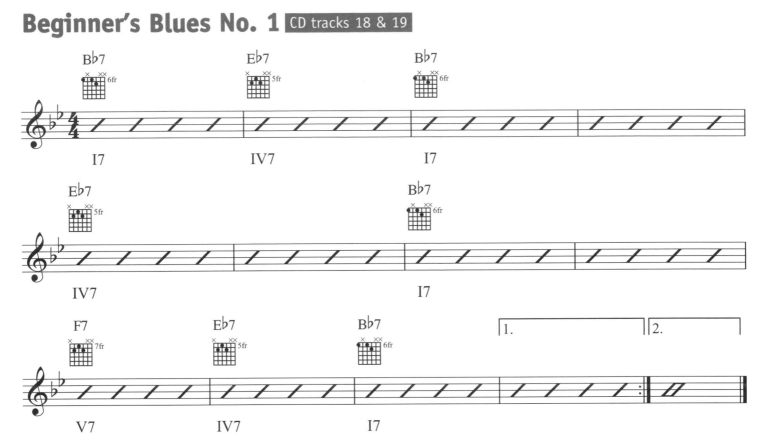

This is almost as simple as the blues can get. Now let's dress it up a bit with some II–V changes:

Beginner's Blues No. 2 CD tracks 20 & 21

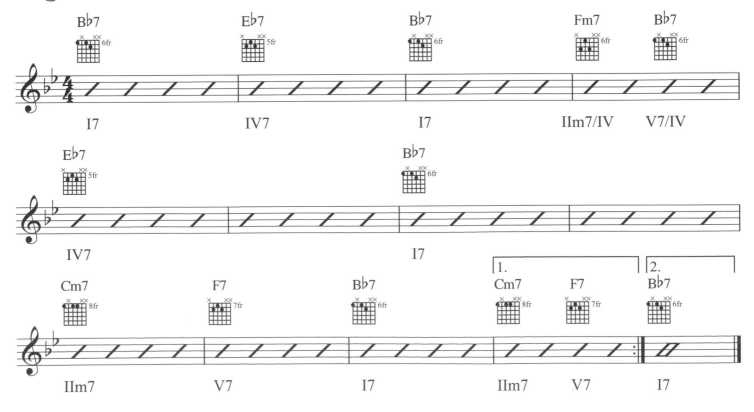

Let's take it further. Do you remember the chromatic VI7 chord from our cycle of fifths (see page 13)? Let's stick it in front of our II–V progression. The VI7 chord, being a dominant 7th, *wants* to resolve to II (up a fourth), which takes us nicely to V7, which in turn *wants* to resolve to the I chord.

Beginner's Blues No. 3 CD tracks 22 & 23

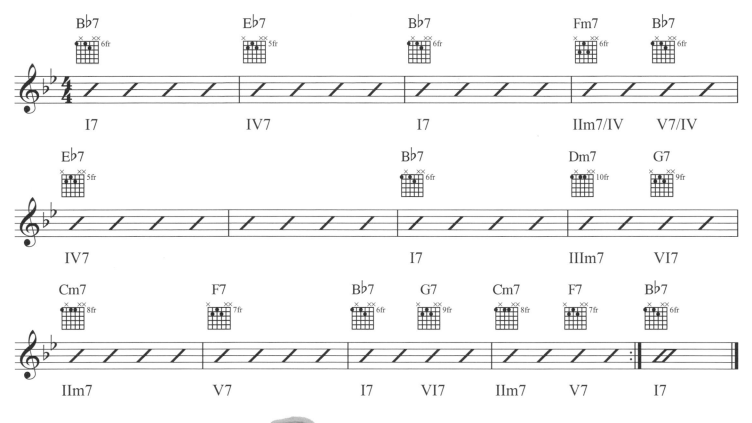

The next sequence takes this idea even further still. In a cyclic sequence (such as Dm7–G7–Cm7–F7) any chord can be turned into a dominant 7th; it's really a matter of taste and fitting with the tune.

The cycle of fifths has such a strong sound that we can start as early as we like, hence the A7 chord in measure 7 below, which is actually pretty far removed from the key of B♭.

Advanced Beginner's Blues CD tracks 24 & 25

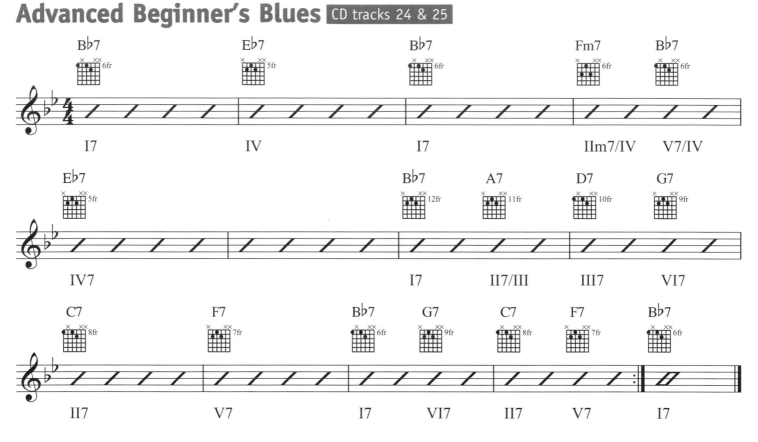

So far, we've left major 7th chords out of the picture—they don't usually work in a blues context (try it and see!).

The following chord sequences use major 7th chords, as well as a fair dose of II–V action. (The harmonic analyses start to get a little cluttered at this point, so see if you can figure out the roman numerals for yourself.)

Fruit Smoothie CD tracks 26 & 27

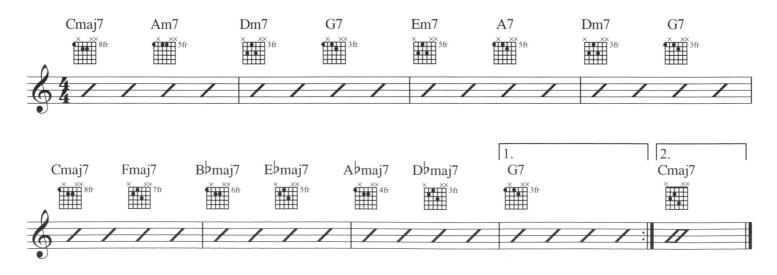

All Is Well CD tracks 28 & 29

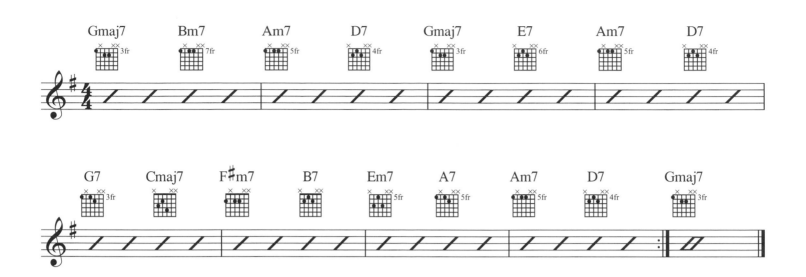

The beauty of the shapes you've just learned is in their simplicity. Unlike open chords, there's no unnecessary *clutter*. The next thing we're going to look at is adding flavor to these chords through the addition of various types of fifths and upper extensions such as ninths and thirteenths. Since open shapes often contain the fifth more than once, how do we turn them into augmented fifths? Raising just one of them creates a clash with the other. Raising both of them can result in an impossible shape and an unbalanced sound. Fortunately, the shapes you've just learned contain no unnecessary notes and can therefore be extended easily.

Rather than getting bogged down in theory, let's take a practical approach and look at the physical possibilities of adding a note to each of these six shapes. The top strings have been unused so far; let's look at what happens when we bring the B string into play. Here are all the possibilities that make any musical sense (though some are rarely used). Each possibility combines one of the basic shapes (black dots) with *one* possible extension (*one* of the gray dots).

Roots on the Sixth String

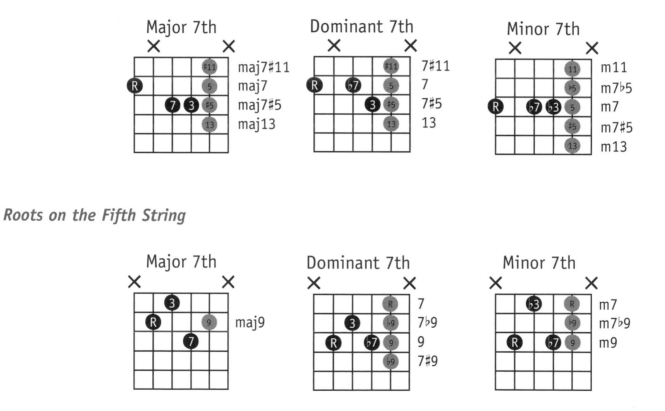

Roots on the Fifth String

Some of these extensions have *enharmonic* (interchangeable) names. The ♯11 is the same pitch as the ♭5, and the ♯5 is the same as a ♭13. This can get bit complicated, so I won't go into the theory behind which name to use and when, but I'll stick to the way they are most commonly applied.

Where the "extension" is a natural fifth (5) or doubled root (R), it isn't mentioned in the chord name as it isn't really an extension; the assumption is that a fifth is natural unless otherwise stated.

You'll notice that some of the shapes in the following pieces contain a curved line joining two or three notes. This is called a *bar* and means that you play several notes with the same finger. (If you're not sure how to do this, look ahead to page 32.)

Now let's see what we can do with some of these extended shapes. Don't worry about the theory at this point, just play through the following pieces and get comfortable with some of the ways we can connect these chords.

Big Bossa Man CD tracks 30 & 31

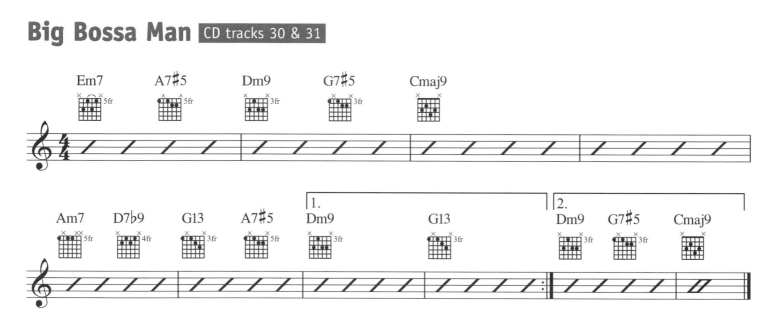

Let's Swing Again CD tracks 32 & 33

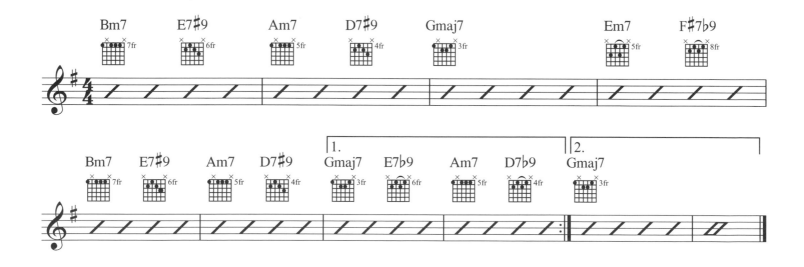

Dirty Dozen CD tracks 34 & 35

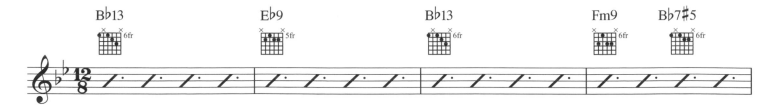

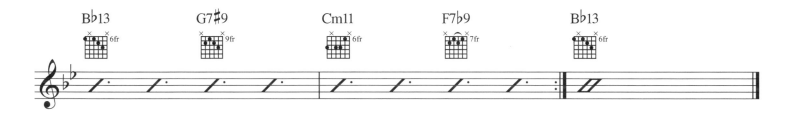

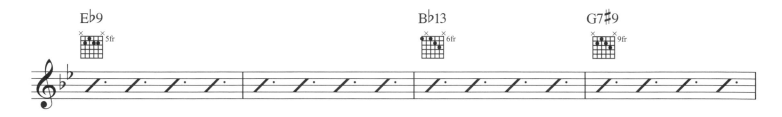

Stop Bossing CD tracks 36 & 37

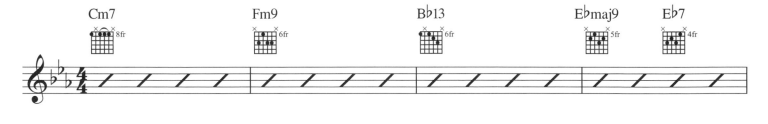

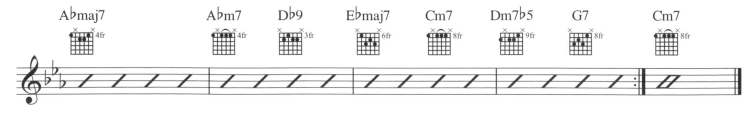

If you're awake, you'll have noticed a new shape in "Stop Bossing":

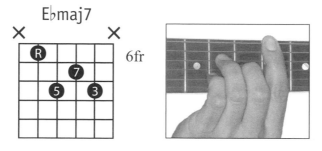

E♭maj7

This is a new voicing that breaks the rules I set down a few pages ago. Such is life...E♭maj9 just didn't sound right, and the alternative would have been either a basic three-note voicing (where's the B string gone?) or a leap up to the eleventh fret, neither of which would have been musical. This well-balanced voicing (root, fifth, seventh, third) is useful not only in jazz but in all sorts of jazz-influenced pop situations. For this reason I call them "semi-jazz" voicings. (See page 46 for more of these.)

I hope you've noticed something that's starting to happen with these chord sequences: the notes on the B string are connecting melodically. Even if you're just providing chords behind a singer or other solo instrument, the chords will be so much more satisfying if this *voice leading* is going on. We can also use this type of motion to create *chord melodies,* where you're playing chords and a melody at the same time. However, you'll need a few more chords at your disposal before you can apply this to any tune.

These last few examples all used chords with upper extensions (ninths, elevenths, and thirteenths). The word *tension* is often used to describe these notes; they generally sound as though they want to resolve to another note. This is particularly true with dominant 7th chords, because the chord itself wants to resolve, too. Try playing these two chords:

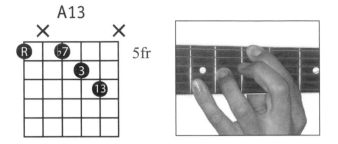

Let each chord ring. Which sounds more stable? Would you agree that they both sound as though they want to go somewhere else, but the A7#5 especially? Try resolving both chords to either of these:

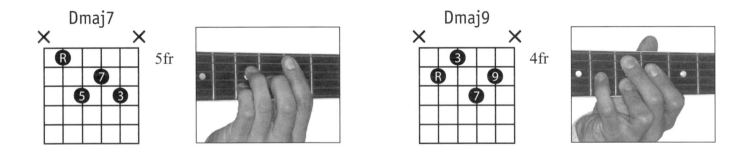

Mmm... nice. A simple V–I progression—the perfect cadence again. The reason that the A7#5 sounds more in need of resolution is that the raised fifth (F) is a chromatic note: it doesn't belong to D major.

No, I haven't decided to turn this book into a self-help manual on stress relief! What I'm talking about here is how to decide whether to use natural or altered (chromatic) tensions. We have two types of tensions available for use with dominant 7th chords:

Natural Tensions	Altered Tensions
9	♭9
13	♯9
5	♯5 or ♭13
♭5 or ♯11	♭5 or ♯11

No, that's not a misprint. The lowered fifth (or raised eleventh) can be considered as either natural or altered. Don't ask why, just trust me at this point. The natural fifth is arguably not a "tension" note as it's part of the basic four-note chord, but I think it's simpler to think of it as an extension, as you'd generally only want either a natural or raised fifth present, not both.

So, when can you use a natural tension and when can you an use an altered tension? Here's a good general rule:

With a functional dominant (a V–I progression, resolving up a fourth), use either type according to taste. With a static (non-resolving) dominant, use natural tensions only.

Confused? Let's clarify this with the following examples:

Basic Bossa CD tracks 38 & 39

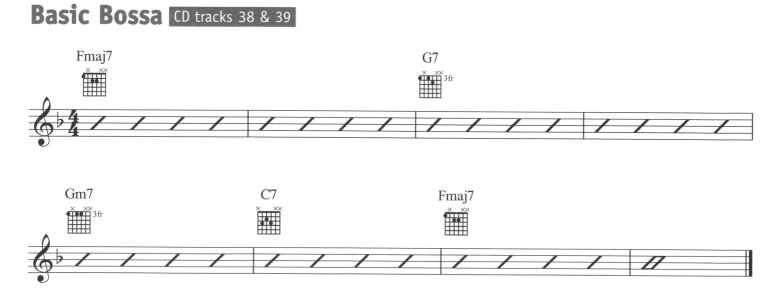

This sequence contains two dominant 7th chords: G7 and C7. The G7 is a *static* dominant: it does not resolve. The C7 is a *functional* dominant: it resolves to F. According to the above rule, we can use natural tensions on both of them:

Natural Bossa CD tracks 40 & 41

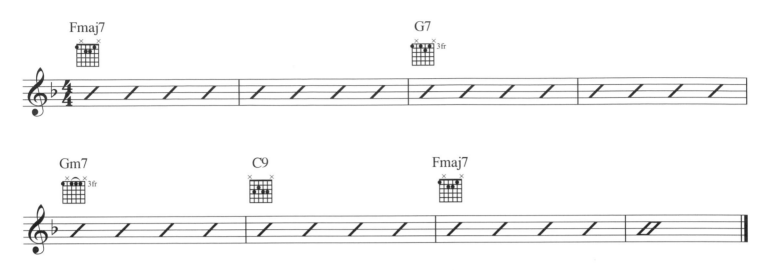

Notice that I'm now using the B string in all of these chords. If you think of each string as a "voice," it's generally not good to have voices appearing and disappearing at random.

This sequence sounds fine, but perhaps a bit dull. As the C9 is a functional dominant, we can spice it up with some altered tensions. In this case, the lowered ninth joins up with the other chords nicely to produce a chromatically descending line on the B string (D–D♭–C):

Unnatural Bossa CD tracks 42 & 43

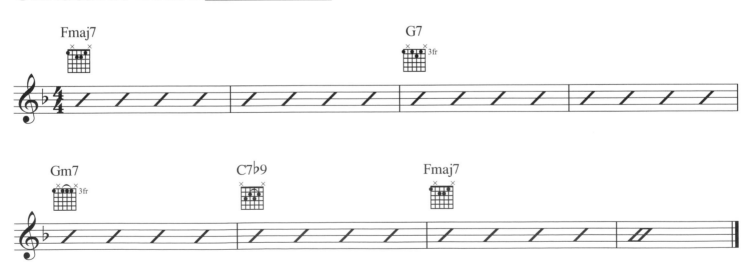

Lovely. Now here's my chance to prove the point about the lowered fifth working with a static dominant. Here it is with our G7:

Cookin' Bossa CD tracks 44 & 45

Bar chords: the inevitable chapter

So far, we've looked at a few open chords that aren't moveable and some jazz voicings that are. Jazz chords don't cover every situation—sometimes only plain major and minor chords will do, when you *want* a full, ringing sound with lots of notes

doubled. So how can we take these open chords all over the neck? If you just want to be able to play three-chord songs in a variety of keys, a *capo* is the simplest option:

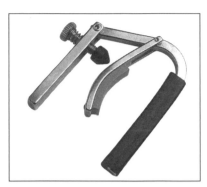  

This handy device clamps around the neck at any fret and effectively raises the pitch of the whole instrument. So, playing an open A-chord shape with a capo at the first fret (one semitone up) gives you a B♭ chord, and so on. If you want to use a capo to play a simple song in a strange key, you can use the transposition chart on page 47 to find a capo position that will work. For example, if you need B♭, E♭, and F, you can use the shapes for G, C, and D (respectively) with the capo at the third fret.

I'm not going to say much more about using the capo because there isn't much more to say! By all means get one, play around with it and see what comes out. The capo can be particularly effective

higher up the neck, where it effectively turns the guitar into a different instrument. Listen to "Here Comes The Sun" by the Beatles and you'll see what I mean.

However, if you want the flexibility of being able to play all sorts of big, ringy chords all over the neck in all keys without stopping to move the capo, there's only one answer: *bar chords*. You know at least one already (F), which I included among the "easy chords" on page 9.

The principle is simple: One finger (almost always the first finger) is pressed down across all six strings at once.

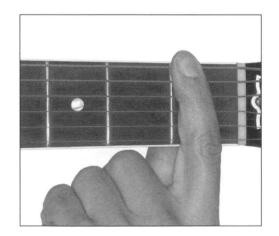

This is called a *full bar*. Later, we'll look at some *half bar* shapes, but we'll start with the full bar, as it takes a bit of work at first. The aim is to raise the pitch of all six strings, just like a capo. Don't worry if you get a bit of buzz at first; this will improve as

your fingers get stronger. It may also be a bit painful. If this is the case, don't spend hours practicing bar chords at first; keep them on as a "back burner" project and you'll get there in the end.

Once the first finger is in place, you have three fingers left with which you can play more or less any chord shape. Our first bar chords are going to be based on these simple open chords from page 9:

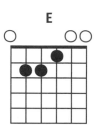

E

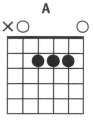

A

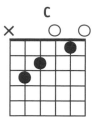

C

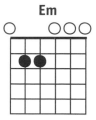

Em

Am

For example, we can bar the first fret and play an E shape, one fret up, with the remaining fingers:

F

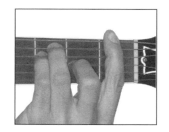

As *every note* of the E chord has now been raised by a semitone, the resulting chord is an F. Raising an

Em by one semitone gives us Fm; raising a C by a tone (two frets) gives us an alternative D shape.

Fm

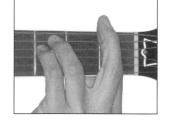

D

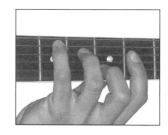

Here are a few more:

B♭

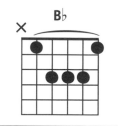

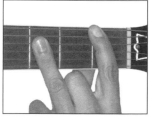

B

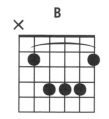

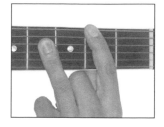

Bm

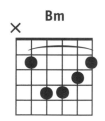

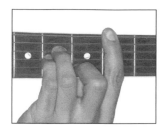

OK, let's see what we can do with these bar chords.

Slippery Punk CD tracks 46 & 47

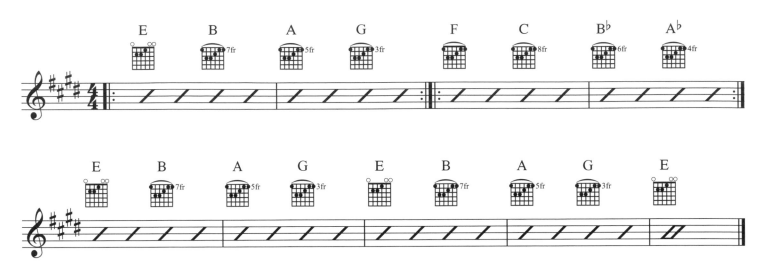

Taking a chord shape and sliding it around like this is a million miles away from the smooth voice-leading concept of the previous chapter, but then that's what makes it sound like punk rock rather than jazz!

Now let's combine some bar chord shapes to give us a chord progression in the otherwise impossible key of A♭ minor.

Coalface Piano Disaster* CD tracks 48 & 49

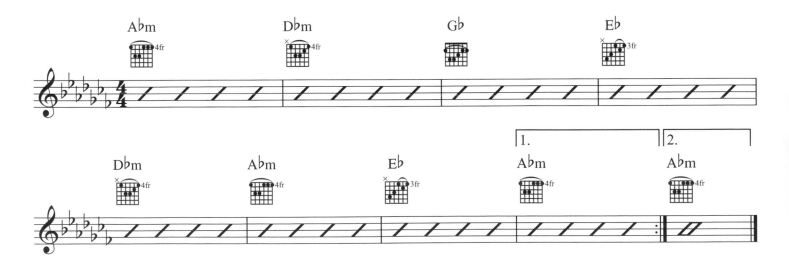

* *What do you get if you drop a piano down a mine shaft? A flat minor.*

Here's a chord progression that could be played using just our basic chords, but takes on a completely different character using bar chords.

Sweet 'n' High CD tracks 50 & 51

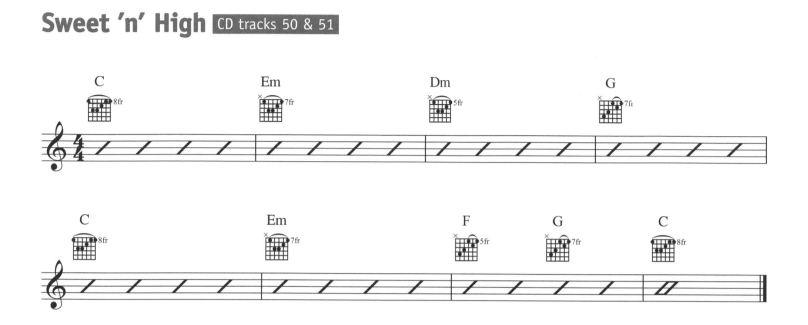

Here's a chord sequence that would sound entirely different with open chords. With no open strings, you can use heavy left-hand damping to produce a choppy, staccato effect.

Behind Bars CD tracks 52 & 53

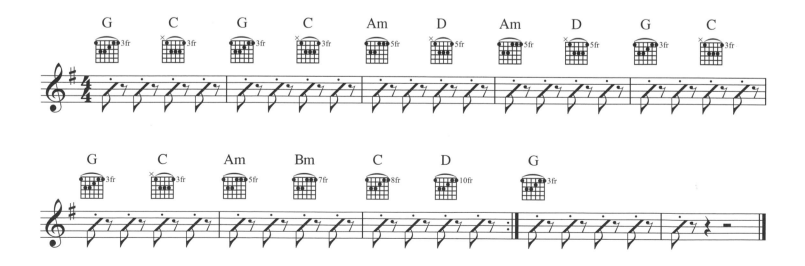

Here's a funky minor blues using some minor 7th bar chords.

When Gary Met Larry CD tracks 54 & 55

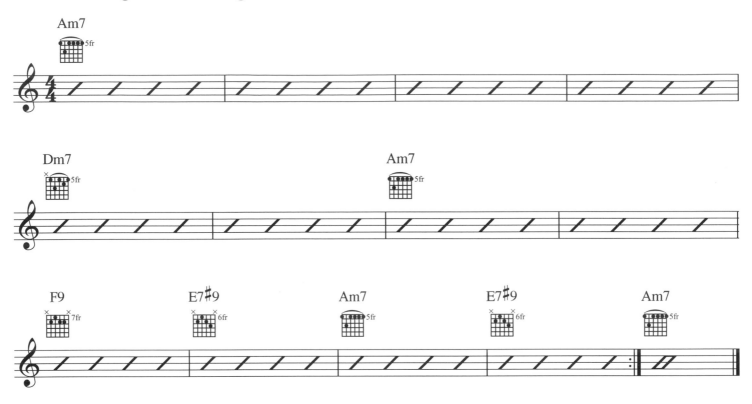

No prizes for spotting the jazz voicings that I've mixed in here. Yes, they *can* live together. While we're at it, notice that the F9 is a static chord with a natural tension (ninth), whereas the E7 chord resolves to Am, so we can use a chromatic tension (raised ninth).

Before we head back over to the dark side to look at some more jazz chords, here's a classic cycle of fifths progression that's been used in countless tunes, using some bar chords and some jazz voicings:

Mooning CD tracks 56 & 57

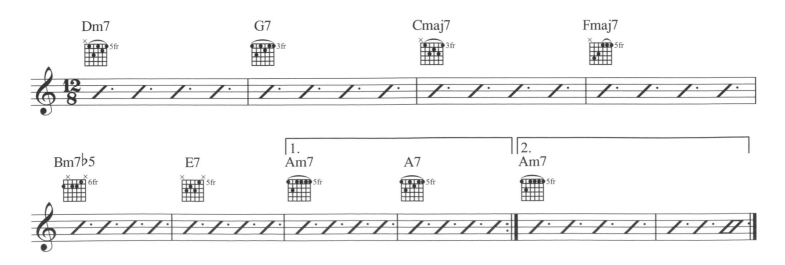

Let's look at what happens if we add extensions to our jazz chords on the top E string, too. We'll confine this to dominant 7th chords for the moment.

Roots on the Sixth String

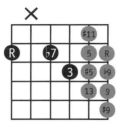

On one level, this gives us a bewildering variety of possible chords. A quick glance should show you that not all of them are even physically playable! Let's narrow down the possibilities by leaving out the *mixed tension* chords for now, that is to say, we'll exclude the possibility of natural and altered tensions within the same chord. (Ultimately these are useful and uniquely hip-sounding chords, but you need to be able to walk before you can run!) As before, the lowered fifth (raised eleventh) can be considered either natural or altered (chromatic); the natural fifth, being a basic chord tone, will work with an altered ninth.

Roots on the Fifth String

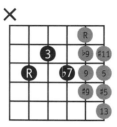

The other way to make these chords more manageable is to leave out the root—let the bass player take care of it. (He'll thank you for not getting in his way.)

We're actually left with just a handful of incredibly useful shapes. Let's group the possibilities according to the the theoretical root (even though we're not playing it) and whether they contain natural or altered tensions.

Roots on the Sixth String

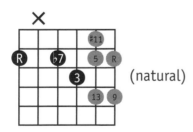 (natural)

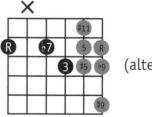 (altered)

Roots on the Fifth String

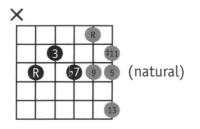 (natural)

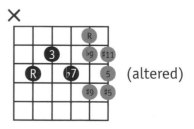 (altered)

That's enough theorizing for one chapter! Let's have a look at some of the shapes we can make with these combinations. A jazz blues makes the best vehicle for putting them into action.

Natural-Tension Blues `CD tracks 58 & 59`

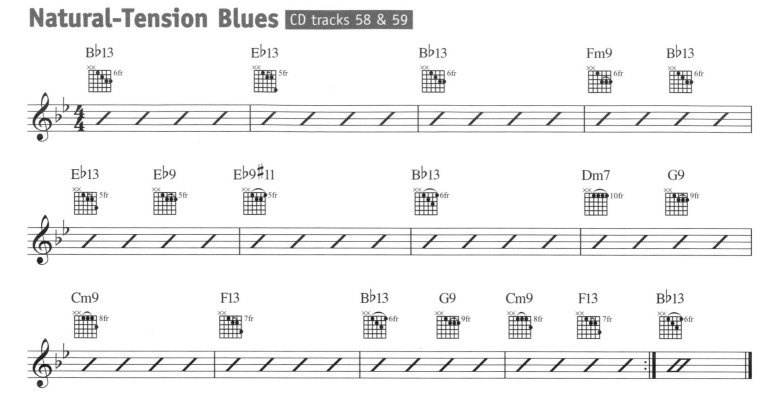

We can dress up all the functional dominants in this progression with altered tensions and suddenly it's *real* jazz!

Altered-Tension Blues `CD tracks 60 & 61`

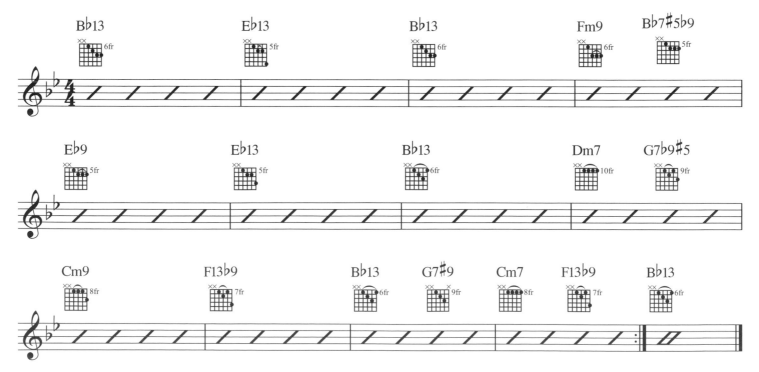

OK, so I cheated. F13♭9 is a mixed-tension chord. Sounds good, doesn't it? Notice also that there are two different voicings of B♭13 in both of the above examples: one with a ninth, and one without. It's a matter of melodic taste.

Here's a soulful minor blues number full of altered tensions. There are some new shapes here, but nothing you can't get under your fingers at this point!

Minor Quibble CD tracks 62 & 63

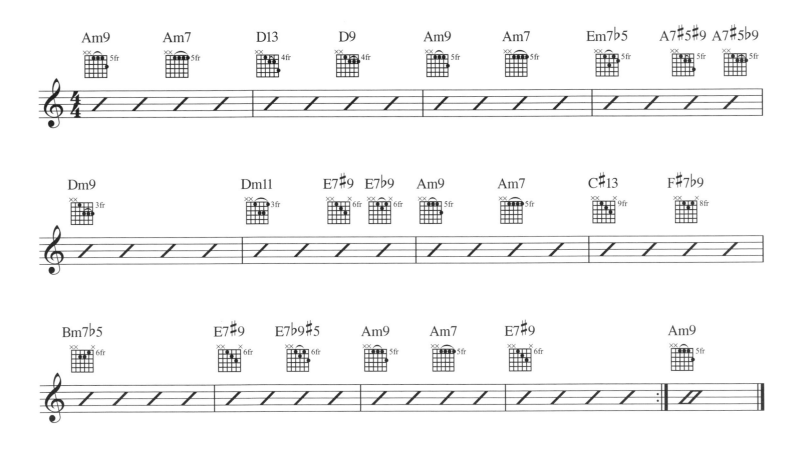

Let's take this about as far we can with a Latin workout based on the cycle of fifths. I've used both natural- and altered-tension chords. Get them under your fingers to the point where you can really hear the difference. There are some new shapes here, too.

The first version on the CD is at a slower, "starter" tempo with percussion only. When you've mastered all the changes you can turn up the heat and play the fast version with the full band.

Latin Homework CD tracks 64 & 65 (slow)   CD tracks 66 & 67 (fast)

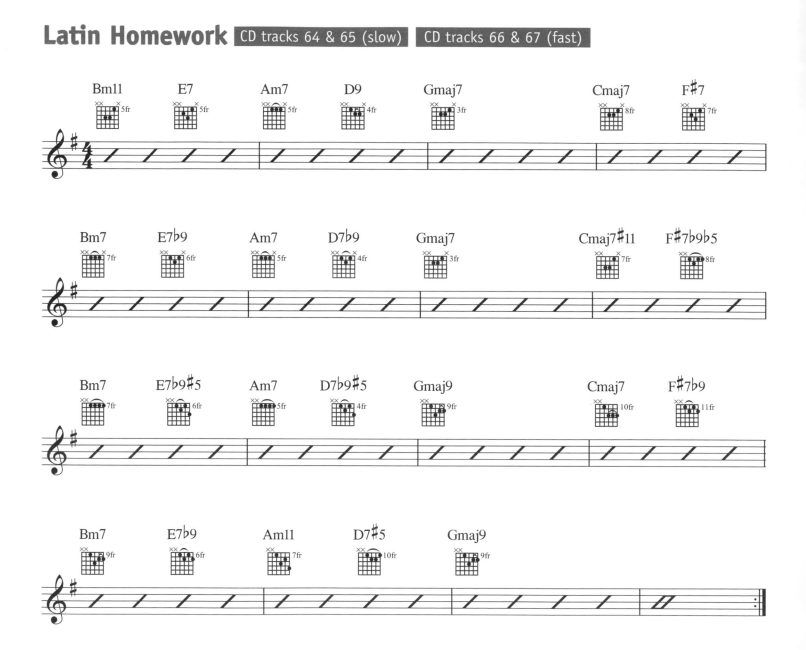

So far, all of the chords in this book have had the root note in the bass (except the chords in the last chapter, which had no real bass notes at all.) Let's consider some chords with the third in the bass.

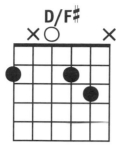

D/F♯

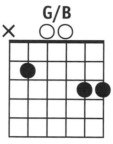

G/B

This D chord now has an F♯ (the third) in the bass. Compare it to a standard open D chord and savor the difference. Would you agree that D/F♯ ("D over F♯" or "D with an F♯ in the bass") sounds less stable, as though it wants to lead somewhere else?

These chords are called *inversions;* jazz and rock musicians often call them *slash chords,* not because of any association with the Guns 'n' Roses guitarist, but because they are written with a forward slash. They are useful for connecting the bass notes in a simple chord sequence to create a bassline moving by step. Consider the sequence C–G–Am. Now change the G to G/B and try both versions. Doesn't the G/B version sound more "connected"? Now try changing Em–D–G to Em–D/F♯–G.

The above chords are both *first* inversions. Taking the G chord as an example, the notes in the chord are G (root), B (third), and D (fifth). The other possible inversion would be G/D (with the fifth in the bass)—this would be called the *second* inversion. A G7 chord (G–B–D–F) with F in the bass (G7/F) would be the third inversion, and so on.

Enough big words already, let's see some inversions in action.

All Joined Up CD tracks 68 & 69

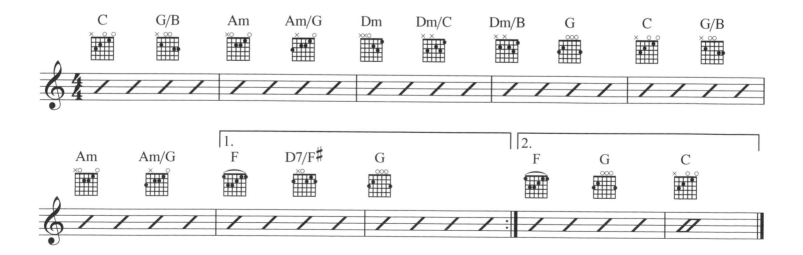

Forward Slash CD tracks 70 & 71

All the chords we've seen so far in this book, including inversions, have included a third. What happens if we replace this note with the perfect fourth?

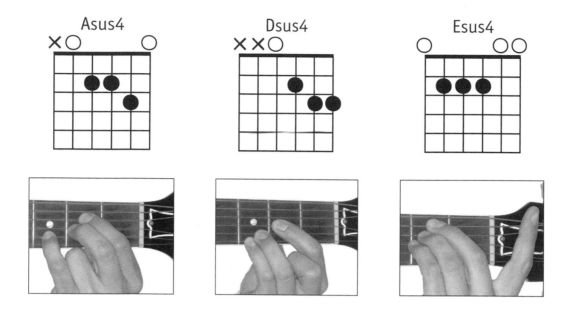

These are called *suspended* (or "sus") chords. They sound as though they literally *hang*, with the fourth wanting to resolve. Play the straight major chord after each of these and experience the feeling of release as the suspended fourth resolves to the third in this next tune.

Hangin' On CD tracks 72 & 73

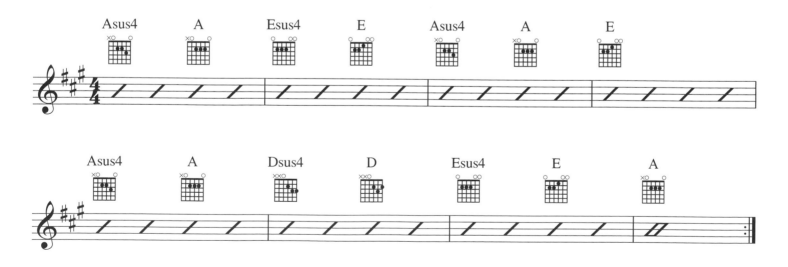

We've covered lots of different types of chords, useful for all sorts of musical situations. The following piece rolls them all together into a ball...

Signing Off CD tracks 74 & 75

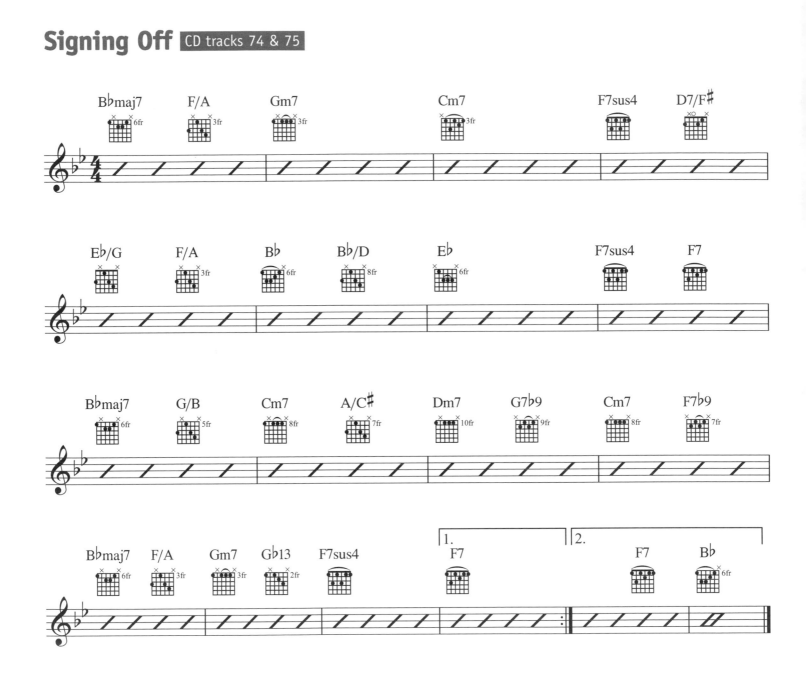

Let's round up the various basic voicings we've used throughout the book and use them to harmonize the major scale. This should help put the knowledge into context and act as a handy point of reference.

Jazz Voicings (root–7th–3rd–5th)—Roots on the Sixth String—Key of F major

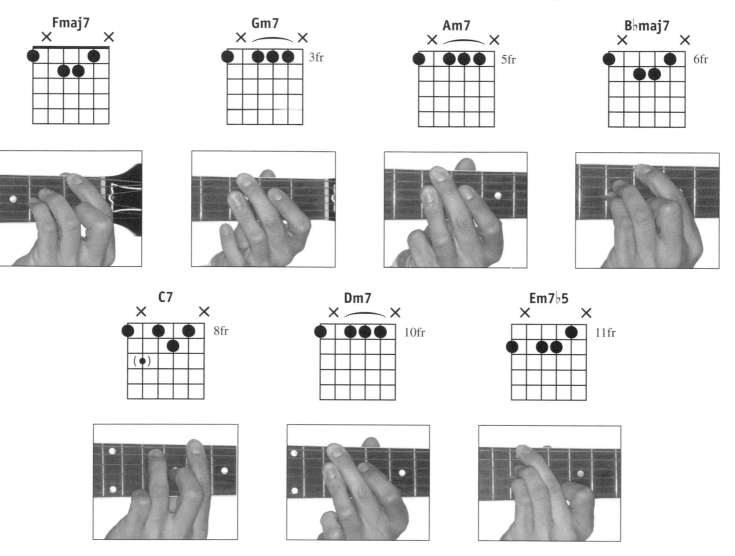

Jazz Voicings (root–3rd–7th–9th)—Roots on the Fifth String—Key of C major

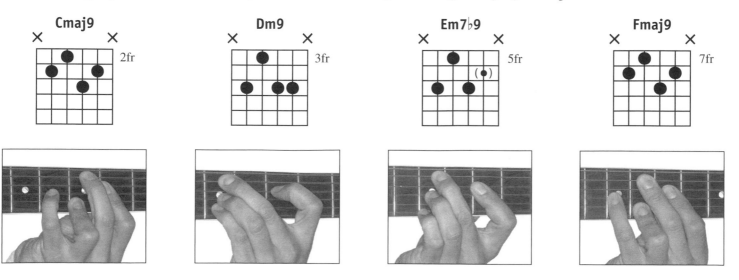

G9

Am9

Bm7♭9

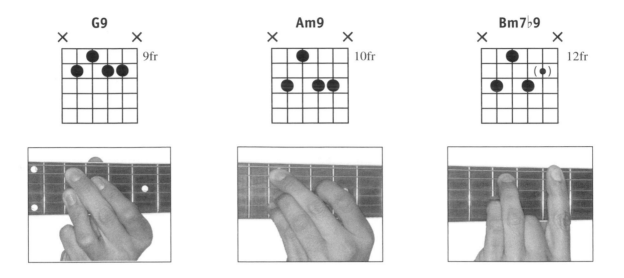

Semi-Jazz Voicings (root–5th–7th–3rd)—Roots on the Fifth String—Key of B♭ major

B♭maj7

Cm7

Dm7

E♭maj7

F7

Gm7

Am7♭5

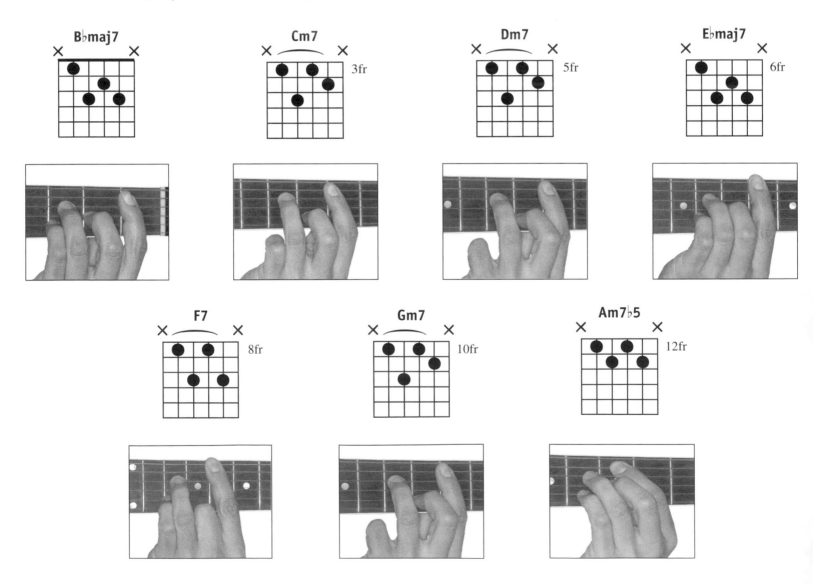

You can use this handy table to help you transpose any chord progression to any key. Simply find the original key (the I chord) in the first column and look down that column to find the new key. The row for this new key will then contain all your transposed chords. For example, to transpose a song from D to F, find all your chords in the row for the key of D, then use the corresponding chords in the row for the key of F (D becomes F, G becomes B♭, A becomes C, and so on).

Remember to transfer the chord qualities of chromatic chords and retain any extensions and alterations. A III7#9#5 – VI7#5#9 – II7♭9#5 – V7#5♭9 – Imaj9 in C, which is E7#9#5 – A7#5#9 – D7♭9#5 – G7#5♭9 – Cmaj9, becomes G7#9#5 – C7#5#9 – F7♭9#5 – B♭7#5♭9 – E♭maj9 in key of E♭. Got it?

I		IIm		IIIm	IV		V		VIm		VII°
C	C#/D♭	Dm	D#/E♭	Em	F	F#/G♭	G	G#/A♭	Am	A#/B♭	B°
C#/D♭	D	D#/E♭m	E	Fm	F#/G♭	G	G#/A♭	A	A#/B♭m	B	C°
D	D#/E♭	Em	F	F#m	G	G#/A♭	A	A#/B♭	Bm	C	C#°
D#/E♭	E	Fm	F#/G♭	Gm	G#/A♭	A	A#/B♭	B	C	C#/D♭	D
E	F	F#m	G	G#m	A	A#/B♭	B	C	C#m	D	D#°
F	F#/G♭	Gm	G#/A♭	Am	B♭	B	C	C#/D♭	Dm	D#/E♭	E°
F#/G♭	G	G#/A♭m	A	A#/B♭m	B	C	C#/D♭	D	D#/E♭m	E	F°
G	G#/A♭	Am	A#/B♭	Bm	C	C#/D♭	D	D#/E♭	Em	F	F#°
G#/A♭	A	A#/B♭m	B	C	C#/D♭	D	D#/E♭	E	Fm	F#/G♭	G°
A	A#/B♭	Bm	C	C#m	D	D#/E♭	E	F	F#m	G	G#°
A#/B♭	B	Cm	C#/D♭	Dm	D#/E♭	E	F	F#/G♭	Gm	G#/A♭	A°
B	C	C#m	D	D#m	E	F	F#	G	G#m	A	A#°

If you've played through everything in this book, you will have substantially increased your knowledge of guitar chords and the things you can do with them. There are many more advanced books which you may find useful if you want to explore harmony and theory at a deeper level.

Appleby, Amy. *Start Reading Music.* New York: Amsco 1992. A proven method to mastering sightreading basics. Whether you are an instrumentalist, singer, or composer, you can take a giant leap forward by learning to read music.

Appleby, Amy, and Peter Pickow. *The Guitarist's Handbook.* New York: Amsco 2002. Five guitar reference books in one handy volume: Guitar Owner's Manual, Music Theory For Guitarists, Guitar Scale Dictionary, Guitar Chord Dictionary, and Guitar Manuscript Paper. For both acoustic and electric guitarists.

The Complete Guitar Player Songbook, Omnibus Edition 2. New York: Amsco 2004. This compilation of three new Complete Guitar Player songbooks contains over 100 songs written by such great songwriters as Bob Dylan, Paul Simon, Elton John, Cat Stevens, John Denver, and many others. Full lyrics are given for each song.

Dineen, Joe, and Mark Bridges. *The Gig Bag Book of Guitar Complete.* New York: Amsco 2001. A sampler of The Gig Bag Book Of Scales, Arpeggios, and Tab Chords. Each two-page spread illustrates a scale with corresponding arpeggio and chords.

Every Musician's Handbook. New York: Amsco 1984. This pocket-sized resource covers rules of harmony, counterpoint, and orchestration. With sections on scales, keys, and chords, plus a musical term glossary.

Lozano, Ed. *Easy Blues Songbook.* New York: Amsco 1997. Learn the art of blues playing by jamming along to the actual tunes made famous by authentic blues artists. Fourteen tunes arranged for easy guitar with note-for-note transcriptions in standard notation and tablature.

Lozano, Ed, and Joe Dineen. *Mastering Modes For Guitar.* New York: Amsco 2002. This practical guide unlocks the mystery behind the construction and application of over 60 modes. Includes special sections on advanced and world scales. All of the examples are demonstrated on the accompanying CD.

Salvador, Sal. *Single String Studies For Guitar.* Miami: Belwin 1966. Simply the best book for alternate picking. A complete study of single string exercises designed to build technique and control.

Scharfglass, Matt. *The Gig Bag Book of Practical Pentatonics For All Guitarists.* New York: Amsco 2000. The ultimate compact reference book of pentatonic scales (five-note minor and major scales) and how to use them. Packed with over 400 riffs and examples; also includes a section on theory and more.

Scharfglass, Matt. *You Can Do It: Play Guitar Dammit!* New York: Amsco 2004. This proven method will have you spinning off chords, riffs, and solos in as little time as possible. Includes a specially designed CD with demonstrations of all the music examples plus additional backup tracks.

Willard, Jerry, editor and arranger. *Fifty Easy Classical Guitar Pieces.* New York: Amsco 2004. Contains a delightful repertory of pieces for the beginning or intermediate player, drawn from all periods of classical guitar literature. Includes a full-length CD of all the pieces performed by the author. Learn pieces by Sor, Carulli, Giuliani, Dowland, Bach, DeVisee, and many more.